AN IDEAS INTO ACTION GUIDEBOOK

Keeping Your Career On Track

Twenty Success Strategies

IDEAS INTO ACTION GUIDEBOOKS

Aimed at managers and executives who are concerned with their own and others' development, each guidebook in this series gives specific advice on how to complete a developmental task or solve a leadership problem.

LEAD CONTRIBUTORS	Craig Chappelow
	Jean Brittain Leslie
CONTRIBUTORS	Michael M. Lombardo
	Morgan W. McCall, Jr.
	Cynthia D. McCauley
	Ann M. Morrison
	Ellen Van Velsor
	Randall P. White
GUIDEBOOK ADVISORY GROUP	Victoria A. Guthrie
	Cynthia D. McCauley
	Russ S. Moxley
DIRECTOR OF PUBLICATIONS	Martin Wilcox
EDITOR	Peter Scisco
DESIGN AND LAYOUT	Joanne Ferguson
CONTRIBUTING ARTISTS	Laura J. Gibson
	Chris Wilson, 29 & Company

CCL No. 408
ISBN No. 1-882197-61-5

CENTER FOR CREATIVE LEADERSHIP
POST OFFICE BOX 26300
GREENSBORO, NORTH CAROLINA 27438-6300
336-288-7210 • WWW.CCL.ORG/PUBLICATIONS

Keeping Your Career On Track

Twenty Success Strategies

Craig Chappelow and Jean Brittain Leslie

Center for
Creative
Leadership

NORTH AMERICA EUROPE ASIA

www.ccl.org

THE IDEAS INTO ACTION GUIDEBOOK SERIES

This series of guidebooks draws on the practical knowledge that the Center for Creative Leadership (CCL®) has generated in the course of more than thirty years of research and educational activity conducted in partnership with hundreds of thousands of managers and executives. Much of this knowledge is shared—in a way that is distinct from the typical university department, professional association, or consultancy. CCL is not simply a collection of individual experts, although the individual credentials of its staff are impressive; rather it is a community, with its members holding certain principles in common and working together to understand and generate practical responses to today's leadership and organizational challenges.

The purpose of the series is to provide managers with specific advice on how to complete a developmental task or solve a leadership challenge. In doing that, the series carries out CCL's mission to advance the understanding, practice, and development of leadership for the benefit of society worldwide. We think you will find the Ideas Into Action Guidebooks an important addition to your leadership toolkit.

Table of Contents

EXECUTIVE BRIEF

Managers who achieve significant professional goals don't often worry about career derailment. But complacency isn't the same as continued success. Many high-performing executives have one or more blind spots that they ignore as long as they meet their business goals. The traps that lead to derailment can usually be found among five leadership competencies: interpersonal relationships, building and leading a team, getting results, adapting to change, and having a broad functional orientation. Managers who rely on any of these skills at the expense of the others or who neglect these skills when promoted from a technical to a managerial role can sidetrack their career. Leadership success—achieving it and continuing it—depends heavily on a manager's developing and using each of these skills.

The Bad News: Derailment Happens

Since 1983 the Center for Creative Leadership (CCL) has studied executive derailment across North America and Europe. By comparing successful managers to those who derail, CCL has identified specific factors that lead to success and other factors that force once-successful careers off the track. Managers who are aware of those factors and conduct an honest self-assessment of their leadership skills can go a long way toward keeping a career headed in the right direction.

What does CCL mean by "success" and "derailment"? Its research defines a successful manager as one who has reached at least the general management level and who, in the eyes of senior executives, remains a likely candidate for promotion. A derailed manager is one who, having reached the general manager level, is fired, demoted, or reaches a career plateau. It's important to note that organizations saw the derailed managers as having high potential for advancement, as having impressive track records, and holding a solidly established leadership position—until they derailed. Derailment doesn't refer to individuals who have topped out in their company's hierarchy or to managers who elect to stay at a particular level.

Five key characteristics have been observed in derailed executives. Leaders who derail:
1. have problems with interpersonal relationships
2. fail to hire, build, and lead a team
3. fail to meet business objectives
4. are unable or unwilling to change or adapt
5. lack a broad functional orientation.

The Good News: Success Happens Too

Just as there are clear indicators of derailment, there are also key characteristics associated with successful executives. Leaders who succeed:

1. establish strong relationships
2. hire, build, and successfully lead teams
3. have outstanding track records of performance
4. adapt and develop during transitions.

Perhaps you have received feedback about your performance that describes you in similar ways. This guidebook provides strategies for developing these four characteristics of successful leaders.

Interpersonal Skills

The ability to work with others clearly separates those managers who succeed from those who derail. Managers who are described as interpersonally adept—as having the ability to build and manage effective relationships—are routinely described by bosses, peers, and direct reports as being good listeners, collaborative, supportive of others' ideas, trustworthy, and ethical. Consider this story, from CCL's derailment studies, of a manager who displayed a strong sense of connection with people and was seen as building strong relationships:

> *A woman in the office had recently eloped and the department had taken up a collection to purchase a wedding gift for her. The leader*

instructed them to purchase an engraved cake knife because he had received one on his wedding day, and on every "cake occasion" they use this knife and it always reminds him of his wedding day and how much he loved his wife on that day (and still does). The woman was very touched by that sense of emotion and openness and truly appreciated the cake knife more than one could ever expect. I'm sure she felt a little more loyal to her manager as a result.

The most common reason for derailment is the inability to relate to people in productive ways. Derailed managers who could not establish strong relationships are described as insensitive, competitive, dictatorial, critical, easily angered, arrogant, and manipulative.

This story of an executive who ignored the interpersonal elements of leadership illustrates how a manager invites derailment by mishandling interpersonal relationships.

He is a great strategic thinker and has high ethical standards, but he lashes out at people; he can't build trusting relationships. He is very smart, but he achieves superiority through demeaning others. He is abusive, he hits people with intellectual lightning. He instinctively goes after people. Many people have tried to work on this flaw because he has such extraordinary skills, but it seems hopeless.

Developing Interpersonal Skills

One reason that a lack of interpersonal skills figures so large in executive derailment could be that the behavior associated with those skills is so difficult to change. But it's not impossible. Contrary to what some executives think, it doesn't require a "personality transplant." What it does require is an honest assessment of behavior and a plan to improve specific interpersonal behaviors in specific situations.

1 *Pick someone with whom you are motivated to improve your interpersonal relationship.*

Pick a specific place, time, situation, and duration for practicing your new behavior. An example: "I will not interrupt Mary in our Tuesday morning staff meetings during the question and answer period." Don't worry that this strategy seems too small to address such a big problem. The power of this strategy comes from your developing individual plans for interacting with each person with whom you need to improve your relationship and from setting priorities that translate large behavioral changes into manageable bits.

> How would you describe your interpersonal skills? Have your colleagues, boss, peers, direct reports, or customers given you feedback about your approach to interpersonal relationships? What did they say? Do others seem uncomfortable in your meetings? Are you seldom asked for support or do peers and direct reports readily ask for your perspectives and endorsement? Do you anger easily?

Caution:
- Don't set a plan that isn't specific. A plan to "be a better person" is ineffective because it doesn't direct a specific behavior that you can change.
- Don't fall prey to tunnel vision. You may want to focus on your most critical case, but don't forget to set a specific interaction plan for all of the people with whom you have contact.

2 *Build on your existing relationships.*

Scheduling a lunch meeting with each of your direct reports one day each week to get to know them better is a noble idea. But how do they feel about it? Spending lunch breaks with the boss may be the last thing they want to do. You're better off taking advantage of the interactions you already have on a regular basis.

You can make quite a difference in how others view your interpersonal skills by changing your behavior during short, sincere, face-to-face interactions. Be attentive, genuine, and open. Ask for others' opinions, ask how you can help them get their work done, and listen to what they say.

Caution:

- Don't be false or insincere. Don't use an old ice breaker like "How's the family?" unless you're familiar with children's names and even the interests or work of a spouse or significant other. If you ask a question be prepared to listen to the answer.
- Don't force familiarity. Your peers and direct reports may not want to chat with you about their personal lives. Maybe all they want is a more pleasant interaction with you while at work.

3 *Display empathy toward others.*

Your direct reports, your peers, and your boss are all human beings worthy of your respect and empathy. Listen without judging. Don't cut people off in the middle of a sentence. Take the feelings and perspectives of others into account. If you're talking to a direct report be aware of the power relationship between you and the effect it can have on your interaction.

Caution:

- Don't use humor inappropriately. Your closest friend might appreciate your dry wit and sarcastic asides but peers and direct reports may not.
- Don't disclose private conversations. If someone tells you something in confidence, keep it private. If you make private information public you lose credibility and trust, both essential leadership qualities.

4 *Learn to listen.*

Hearing isn't the same as listening. Turn away from your e-mail and the papers on your desk and concentrate on the person in front of you. Separate what you think about the person from what he or she is saying. Ask questions to make sure you understand what's been said. Take notes to help you remember.

Caution:

- Don't be a passive listener. Pay attention. Translate what you hear and don't let it "go in one ear and out the other." Participate in the conversation without monopolizing it.
- Don't drift from the conversation. Stay "in the moment." If the person talking to you says something intriguing, take a note on it and get back to listening.

5 *Collaborate.*

Everyone has different experiences and preferences related to gathering and sharing information, which can lead to challenges in how we collaborate. Be willing to share information and feelings with others (especially peers) to achieve mutually beneficial goals. Provide information clearly and considerately. Involve others in making decisions.

Caution:

- Don't keep your decision-making process secret. If you gather new facts that lead you to a new decision or to change direction, share those facts with others so they can understand how you came to that decision.
- Don't collaborate on everything. Leadership is partly about making decisions and partly about reaching consensus—and having the wisdom to tell the two apart.

Team Leadership

Changing your focus from doing the work to hiring and leading those who do the work is a major step, if not a leap. To successfully make that step you need new skills and an expanded definition of success. The bottom line is still the bottom line, but at the general manager level team leadership is the measure of accomplishment. Successful leaders build and lead effective teams and are described as being good at communicating with the team, motivating the team, delegating, selecting team members who can work together and produce results, and setting clear goals and performance expectations. Consider this story of a manager with effective skills in building and leading a team:

> *Our teamwork was not good despite having a common goal. Communication, feedback, and team behavior were at a low level. The team leader helped set new norms by bringing in an outside facilitator to help team members improve candor and communication. The team agreed on these norms and subsequent meetings supported that view. The leader also established a reward system based on achieving team goals. Teamwork improved quite a bit because team members understood that the team goal was everyone's overriding concern.*

Organizations hire employees because of such characteristics as intellect, independence, drive, decisiveness, and ambition. Organizations typically promote for the same reasons. But when you reach the senior level it's no longer acceptable to get results at any cost. You need to exert more influence and less command and control. Executives who risk derailing can find themselves described as avoiding conflict, failing to motivate others, not sharing credit, and unwilling to delegate.

This story describes an executive whose inability to effectively lead a team had a negative effect on team performance:

The team's task was to develop the organization's new telephone network. It was having difficulties in developing and coordinating the system, so the senior team leader laid down ground rules, in a very threatening way, that all reports had to come to him. Members of the team were not allowed to proceed without consulting him and getting his approval for action. As a result the team's performance declined. Team members became overly competitive. Disagreements hampered communication, which severely delayed system implementation and led to higher maintenance costs at launch.

Developing Skills for Building and Leading an Effective Team

Teams are essential components to many high-performing organizations. If you want to remain successful in your leadership role you have to create and lead teams that can define their missions, can work effectively as a group, and can reach goals. The following strategies will help you build these skills.

What kind of feedback have you received from your colleagues, boss, peers, direct reports, or customers on your ability to build and lead a team? Do they see you as someone who can select the right people for a team? Are you described as being a strong motivator, as someone who can share the task of leadership? Have others described you as being unwilling to delegate responsibility?

6 *Determine what motivates your direct reports.*

It's not always the paycheck. Some workers enjoy collaborating with co-workers, others the freedom to work independently with minimal supervision. Think about times or projects when one of your direct reports worked at his or her highest performance level. Ask team members what motivates them. Record each person's motivating value, then do what you can to create motivational opportunities that match those values.

Caution:
- Don't promise more than you can deliver. If a team member is motivated by the opportunity to get out of a cubicle and into an office, don't promise that office if you can't provide it. Your credibility as a leader is at stake.
- Don't forget intangible rewards. Bonuses and perks are great when possible, but public recognition for handling a tough task is a powerful and sometimes overlooked motivator.

7 *Help your team set a clear mission and be sure that every team member understands it.*

Can you define your team's mission right now? If it's not clear in your own mind, you might be sending mixed signals to your team about the group's direction. You should be able to state the mission for your group in one or two sentences. It should be clear and concise, and developed so that team members can link their tasks to the team's mission.

Caution:
- Don't overuse jargon. Use everyday language that you're comfortable with to define and communicate the team's mission.
- Don't ignore team "norms"—accepted ways of behaving, interacting, and working together. Live the team norms through your own actions. Lead by example.

8 *Hire people who can contribute to your group in diverse ways.*

There is so much in print about racial and gender diversity that we often overlook the benefits of personality diversity and skill diversity. Go for a balanced, complementary team. Analyze your team's goals and determine what kinds of skills, knowledge, and abilities are needed to reach those goals. Interview and examine all potential and current team members for the knowledge, skills, and abilities they bring to bear on the team's tasks. Select or develop team members who match up well with what the team needs and who complement each other in their range of skills.

Caution:
- Don't just hire in your own image. You may have risen from the engineering ranks, but a team of engineers may only exaggerate weaknesses rather than fill gaps. Managers who have trouble leading a team often select people with backgrounds similar to their own.
- Don't ignore input from your team. Solicit advice from team members and involve them in decisions—especially selection—whenever possible.

9 *Deal with problem employees in a direct, timely manner.*

There usually isn't a quick fix for employee-performance problems, and they rarely work themselves out. If a direct report's behavior or lack of skills threatens the success of your team, you want to help your employee improve before another project suffers. Consult with your HR staff if necessary.

Caution:
- Don't confront the employee in question without specific documented examples.
- Don't overreact by firing an employee before attempting some course of performance development.

10 *Empower your team and delegate your authority.*

Allow team members to work on projects that you think they can handle. Increase the complexity of assignments as long as you feel they stand a good chance of succeeding. Give them adequate guidance and follow up with them from time to time to see how they are doing. Ask members to suggest ways to improve how the team does its work.

Caution:
- Don't keep the same team members tied to the same team roles and responsibilities. If team members can't explore new perspectives they may lose commitment to the team and the team's performance will suffer.
- Don't forget to publicly announce and reward the team for accomplishing tasks, passing milestones, or achieving goals.

Getting Results

It's simple. Organizations promote managers who get the job done. But it's not just one job well done—it's a record of consistent exceptional performance that is key to career and leadership success. Successful managers who get results can be described as outstanding performers, having a consistent track record, able to get the job done, steady climbers, and not afraid of responsibility.

This story of a manager illustrates how exceptional leadership skills can be used to meet business objectives and get results.

The goals were already very challenging and then they were moved up again. The leader feared that morale would be adversely affected and that it would hurt our ability to hit the goal. People were skeptical about the original goal. The leader had a meeting with the entire staff. He told them that he felt the goal was achievable and why. He then asked them to pretend it was December 31 and that we had exceeded our goal. He asked them how they felt; how it felt to succeed. The team talked about what they had done during the previous months to achieve the goal. People were pumped up; they realized they could do it. Morale shot up and sustained itself. We exceeded the goal.

Poor performance seems like an obvious derailment factor. After all, if you aren't doing the work, you probably won't keep your job—at least not for long. What's less obvious is how senior executives with successful track records become poor performers. Some managers remain too focused on promotion, concentrating on the job they want next and failing to take care of the business at hand. Executives who derail because they failed to meet business objectives are described as less driven to work hard, self-promoting, easily overwhelmed, failing to follow through, and overly ambitious. Consider this description of a manager who was ineffective at meeting business objectives:

We had a huge project—our biggest. It is late. It has cost hundreds of thousands of dollars because we didn't have needed staff and systems in time. This is her responsibility.

Developing the Ability to Get Results

As you move up the executive ranks to the higher levels of your organization, you must make a shift from an individual contributor role to an influence-based, team-oriented role. Meeting business objectives becomes harder because you have less control over the "nuts and bolts" of the task—you have to implement strategy and accomplish goals by directing and encouraging others to work with the nuts and bolts. The following strategies can help you make that shift and continue your success.

11 *Formalize your performance evaluation criteria.*

Develop specific, measurable criteria with your manager so that you understand how he or she measures your performance. You can also examine company documents—your job description and project mandates, for example—to determine how your organization measures performance. You should understand exactly how your performance will be measured, whether you will have the resources necessary to succeed, what obstacles might lie in your way, and what kind of feedback and evaluation you will receive.

> Could an inability to get results be threatening your career? Have you received feedback from your colleagues, boss, peers, direct reports, or customers that you're not performing as you should be? Do you find it more difficult to get high-quality, timely results now that you've reached a higher leadership position?

Caution:

- Don't rely only on formal performance appraisals. Performance reviews are notoriously incomplete. Seek out feedback from your boss, peers, direct reports, and customers.
- Don't accept performance measurements that are not linked to the company's goals and mission. If you don't see the connection, work with your manager to make the connection clearer.

12 *Develop informal feedback sources.*

Solicit feedback on a routine basis. Periodically ask your manager and others: "Am I working on the right things?" After a meeting, when you are walking back to your office with one of your peers, you might ask: "How do you think that meeting went? What could I have done better?"

Caution:
- Don't ask for feedback before setting your developmental goals. You want feedback that will help you reach your goals, and you can't get that unless you know what those goals are.
- Don't forget to ask family and friends for feedback. People outside of work can provide valuable perspectives on your performance. And because they are outside of work, you can practice new behaviors with family and friends without "political" risk.

13 *Take responsibility for your own development.*

After you've determined what it takes to get results in your current job, assess your skills, knowledge, and abilities. Use the feedback you're getting and your personal assessment to pinpoint where your strengths and weaknesses lie in relation to the demands of your job. Develop a "report card" and give yourself a letter grade for each skill area. Consult with your manager and with your HR department, if possible, for resources to help you develop areas in which you have weaknesses. Track your progress monthly. If you feel that you're not making the gains you'd like, consider hiring an executive coach.

Caution:
- Don't forget to line up support. You need people who can give you feedback about your progress, help you brainstorm solutions to developmental problems, and encourage you when the challenges become difficult.
- Don't refuse assignments because you are afraid to fail. Risks create challenges that stretch you and help you develop new skills. Even failure can be a learning opportunity, although it's not one you want to make into a habit.

14 *Set clear goals and priorities.*

If you wait for total security and perfection you may paralyze your leadership development. You can minimize risks by defining a clear goal, setting priorities, and getting organized. Make sure you understand how your boss and your organization measure performance and then meet those standards through your actions.

Caution:
- Putting in long hours and becoming obsessive about your job performance isn't the same as taking action. A balance between your work life and your personal life will go a long way toward making you more productive and keeping you successful.
- Don't put off what needs to be done. Decide what tasks are most important to accomplishing your goal and take care of those first. Remember the old 80/20 rule: 20 percent of your efforts accomplish 80 percent of your goal. Determine what the 20 percent is for you and set your priorities accordingly.

15 *Focus on the tasks at hand.*

It's all right to focus your developmental plan on skills you will need down the road, but don't forget that your main job is just that—your main job. Focus on what you need to accomplish each day to move closer to achieving personal, team, and organizational goals. Bring jobs to a close. Tie up loose ends. Challenge and develop your direct reports.

Caution:
- Don't forget to think strategically and link your daily work to organizational goals and mission.
- Don't allow yourself to become invisible to upper management by burying yourself in your daily work.

Adaptability and Change

More than ever, the ability to adapt is an important component to executive success. Managers who remain successful become more self-controlling and relaxed over time and remain so during the toughest situations (workforce reductions, for example, or expatriate assignments). Executives characterize managers who maintain flexibility in the face of change as being able to learn the business, learn from mistakes, remain open to feedback, and maintain composure under stress. Consider this story of a manager who remained successful because of an openness to change:

> I used to be a control freak and poor in developing people under me. I was putting too many hours into work and used to wake up at night worrying about business-related issues. We went through an organizational change and I ended up leading a task force on a very important business venture. I made a transformation to become a team player with my new peers. I now behave more like a coach in developing two of my subordinates to take over my responsibilities. I am more relaxed and have become much more of a leader to my organization.

Many managers derail because they are unable or unwilling to adapt. Some of these managers don't change their management style. Other managers resist making changes because their past success indicates to them that they don't need to change and because they fear changes might lead to failure. Such managers are described as avoiding risk, disliking authority figures, closed to feedback, unable to handle pressure, and not strategic in their thinking.

This example of a manager who is unwilling to make changes illustrates how this characteristic can hinder an executive's development and long-term success:

I was coaching her. We had many sessions together where the problems were identified and we tried to come up with an action plan. Some problems she "owned," others she didn't. She really didn't change. She would change for a week or two, then return to baseline.

Developing Adaptability and an Openness to Change

Remaining flexible and adaptable to change may be the most important leadership skill you can develop. The world is changing so quickly on so many fronts—from globalization to e-commerce—that adaptability is rapidly becoming the coin of the executive realm. Further, personal change is as important as external changes. Successful leaders learn from their mistakes, adopt new behaviors, and become lifelong learners. If you struggle with an uneasiness to make changes to your leadership style or to adopt new leadership tactics, try these strategies:

> Are you resistant to change? Do you look for opportunities to learn new skills and perspectives? Do you accept and admit your mistakes and learn from them? What kind of feedback have you received about your adaptability and openness to change?

16 *Get beyond the conflict you have with your boss.*

A new boss brings change to your work, especially if you've grown accustomed to a certain way of doing things. If personal or professional conflicts arise with your new boss (or with your current manager), there are several steps you can take to ease the situation. Make sure you know what your boss expects from you and what you expect from your boss. Handle every matter that affects your relationship with your boss as a priority item. Allow your boss to make mistakes. Keep the communication channel open. Keep on task and be part of the team.

Caution:

- Don't take overt political action by going over your boss's head to get answers to a conflict. Support your boss and his or her agenda in public, but don't confuse support with currying favor. Keep your own perspective and positions—disagree with vigor but respect.
- Don't complain about a lack of direction if your new manager's expectations are not clear. Take the initiative by soliciting feedback, observing who in the organization gets promoted, and talking with peers who have worked with your new boss. That will help you understand what's expected of you.

17 *Identify one specific area where you feel you are stuck in the past.*
Many managers who find trouble in their career have a difficult time adapting to the move from a technical role to a managerial role. Technical roles are objective and specific. They deal with quantifiable tasks, require a hands-on approach, and ask for someone who manages tasks and things. A managerial role is subjective and general, deals with ambiguity, requires a delegating leadership style, and asks for someone who manages people rather than things. Identify what kind of skills are called for in your new role or in the changed environment in which you work, then set goals and round up support for developing those skill areas where you have a weakness.

Caution:

- Don't rely on the strengths that got you the promotion in the first place. By depending on your technical skills you remain weak in the interpersonal skills essential to effective senior leadership.
- Don't allow your misgivings about your chances of success to hold you back from making changes. Making changes is diffi-

cult, even for high achievers. Developing new skills requires you to stretch yourself outside of your "comfort zone."

18 *Understanding the culture of your organization.*

Knowing how your organization thinks is key to aligning yourself with its assumptions and goals and helps you weather the changes that occur in every organization over time. How do decisions get made in your organization? What assumptions does your organization make as it meets challenges and pursues strategy? When change occurs in an organization, such as merger or realignment, managerial roles can be affected. New people can change an organization's culture from the inside; competitive pressures and an evolving business environment can change an organization's culture from the outside.

Caution:
- Don't act in ways that others perceive as too political. To stay successful you have to build trust so that you can build on your interpersonal relationships. If people see you only as a political animal, trust will be hard to build and to maintain.
- Don't hang on to old ways of getting the job done when the organization or the competitive environment changes. One of the hardest tasks a manager takes on when change occurs is moving from the old way to the new way. You can't make that trip unless you leave the past behind.

19 *Seek ongoing feedback.*

Ask for feedback that concentrates on a single situation, describes your behavior in that situation, and communicates the impact of your behavior. Look outside and inside work for feedback sources who are in a position to observe your behavior. Your sources should be people whose opinion you trust and respect and who will support you as you make changes. Ask for feedback that tells you about your process for getting the job done, not just how well or badly you perform.

Caution:

- Don't listen to feedback and then not take action. If you need to make changes, you will have to act on the feedback you receive. Don't dismiss it by blaming other causes.
- Don't ask for opinions. When feedback drifts into the world of interpretation and judgment it ceases to be effective. Ask for factual observations. Ask for feedback that describes the situation in which your behavior was observed, what you did, and how it affected the person giving you the feedback.

20 *Develop self-awareness.*

Recognize your emotional reaction to changes. Maintain standards of honesty and integrity. Be aware of and comfortable with your values; they can be your anchor during times of transition. Don't let success go to your head—your feelings of power can interfere with your willingness to learn from mistakes.

Caution:

- Don't discount the importance of reflection in developing your adaptability toward change. Some managers are resistant to change because they feel under pressure to produce results, which creates in them the perception that reflection is not a relevant use of time. Take the time to review your thoughts and feelings connected to your work. Look for patterns that will help you remain flexible in the face of change.
- Don't forget to modify your leadership style according to the situation. Leadership styles can range from command-and-control, in which you make decisions on your own and pass those decisions to your direct reports, to collaborative, in which you and your team define and solve a problem together.

Success Strategy Checklist

Interpersonal Skills

- ❏ Pick someone with whom you are motivated to improve your interpersonal relationship.
- ❏ Build on your existing relationships.
- ❏ Display empathy toward others.
- ❏ Learn to listen.
- ❏ Collaborate.

Team Leadership

- ❏ Determine what motivates your direct reports.
- ❏ Help your team set a clear mission and be sure that every team member understands it.
- ❏ Hire individuals who can contribute to your group in diverse ways.
- ❏ Deal with problem employees in a direct, timely manner.
- ❏ Empower your team and delegate your authority.

Getting Results

- ❏ Formalize your performance evaluation criteria.
- ❏ Develop informal feedback sources.
- ❏ Take responsibility for your own development.
- ❏ Learn what skills are necessary in the job above you.
- ❏ Focus on the tasks at hand.

Adaptability and Change

- ❏ Get beyond the conflict you have with your boss.
- ❏ Identify one specific area where you feel you are stuck in the past.
- ❏ Understand the culture of your organization.
- ❏ Seek ongoing feedback.
- ❏ Develop self-awareness.

Suggested Readings

Eichinger, R. W., & Lombardo, M. M. (1990). *Twenty-two ways to develop leadership in staff managers.* Greensboro, NC: Center for Creative Leadership.

Leslie, J. B., & Van Velsor, E. (1996). *A look at derailment today: North America and Europe.* Greensboro, NC: Center for Creative Leadership.

Lombardo, M. M., & Eichinger, R. W. (1989). *Eighty-eight assignments for development in place.* Greensboro, NC: Center for Creative Leadership.

McCall, M. W., Jr., Lombardo, M. M., & Morrison, A. M. (1988). *The lessons of experience.* Lexington, MA: Lexington Books.

McCauley, C. D., Moxley, R. S., & Van Velsor, E. (Eds.). (1998). *The Center for Creative Leadership handbook of leadership development.* San Francisco: Jossey-Bass and Center for Creative Leadership.

Van Velsor, E., & Leslie, J. B. (1995). Why executives derail: Perspectives across time and cultures. *Academy of Management Executive, 9*(4), 62-72.

Background

CCL began exploring the dynamics of derailment among North American executives in 1983. Since then, CCL has interviewed hundreds of senior-level executives in scores of companies in the United States and in Europe. Most of the studies have contrasted people who "make it" to the top with those who derail in order to understand the kinds of development needed for senior leadership positions. Results from this research have been used in training programs, assessment instruments, and numerous human-resources initiatives in several organizations.

One of the most remarkable things about the research is that the characteristics of success and derailment have remained fairly constant, even in the context of fast-paced change in organizations and organizational environments, workforce reductions, reengineering and restructuring, the "new employment contract," globalization, and even the rise of the Internet as a business tool.

The lesson, it seems, is that continued leadership success depends on your developing the skills that can move with you as you are promoted from a technical role to a managerial role. Interpersonal skills, adaptability, team leadership, and a focus on results are what keep a leader moving forward, away from the derailment trap.

Key Point Summary

By comparing successful managers to those who derail, the Center for Creative Leadership has identified specific factors that lead to success and other factors that force once-successful careers off the track. Managers who are aware of those factors and conduct an honest self-assessment of their leadership skills can go a long way toward keeping a career headed in the right direction.

A successful manager has reached at least the general man-agement level and, in the eyes of senior executives, remains a likely candidate for promotion. The most commonly mentioned charac-teristics indicating success describe leaders who:

- establish strong relationships
- hire, build, and successfully lead teams
- have outstanding track records of performance
- adapt and develop during transitions.

A derailed manager is one who, having reached the general manager level, is fired, demoted, or reaches a career plateau. In almost every case, a derailed manager exhibits high potential for advancement, holds an impressive track record of results, and holds a solidly established leadership position—until hitting the derailment trap. Five key characteristics have been observed in derailed executives. Leaders who derail:

1. have problems with interpersonal relationships
2. fail to hire, build, and lead a team
3. fail to meet business objectives
4. are unable or unwilling to change or adapt
5. lack a broad functional orientation.

Executives who rise from technical to managerial roles can face challenges in any of these five areas. Fortunately, they can also adopt strategies that take their cue from the descriptions of leaders who enjoy long-term career success. They can avoid the derailment track and work toward long-term success by developing, strengthening, and diversifying their skills among these four leadership qualities:

1. interpersonal skills
2. team leadership
3. achieving business objectives
4. adaptability and openness to change.

None of these success characteristics or fatal flaws is enough to control the outcome of an entire career. Still, most managers who have potentially derailing flaws but the ability to learn and develop can use leadership training, feedback, and developmental assignments to overcome possible career failure and prepare themselves for more senior leadership roles.

Ordering Information

FOR MORE INFORMATION, TO ORDER OTHER
IDEAS INTO ACTION GUIDEBOOKS, OR TO FIND
OUT ABOUT BULK-ORDER DISCOUNTS, PLEASE
CONTACT US BY PHONE AT 336-545-2810 OR
VISIT OUR ONLINE BOOKSTORE AT
WWW.CCL.ORG/GUIDEBOOKS. PREPAYMENT IS
REQUIRED FOR ALL ORDERS UNDER $100.